THE SHIPWRECK OF RMS
HILDEBRAND III

RUTHIE LOCKYER

Published by Ruthie Lockyer

Printed and bound by
Azimuth Print Ltd.
Unit 1, Bowling Hill Business Park
Chipping Sodbury,
Bristol BS37 6JL

Cover design and production by Alan Slingsby and Ruthie Lockyer
with © illustration by Ruthie Lockyer and © photograph courtesy of
Antonio & Carlos Guerra

In memory of my parents

"Barty" Lockyer & John Lockyer

CROSSING THE BAR

Sunset and evening star,
And one clear call for me!
And may there be no moaning of the bar,
When I put out to sea,

But such a tide as moving seems asleep,
Too full for sound and foam,
When that which drew from out the boundless deep
Turns again home.

Twilight and evening bell,
And after that the dark!
And may there be no sadness of farewell,
When I embark;

For tho' from out our bourne of Time and Place
The flood may bear me far,
I hope to see my Pilot face to face
When I have crost the bar.

Alfred Lord Tennyson 1809-1892

The bar referred to is a sandspit or similar promontory at the mouth of a river or harbour where tides have deposited sand over time. To hear the wind and waves moaning off the bar usually means that there is insufficient water to sail over the bar without grounding. Hence the second verse and its reference to a "full tide" or "high water".

CONTENTS

Acknowledgements

The Known Crew

List of Passengers

ACKNOWLEDGEMENTS

Although over fifty years have passed since then, the adventure I experienced as a child still lives in my memory. It seemed exciting at the time, but only because I did not understand its true danger.

Occasionally over the years, I have sought to investigate various aspects of the incident. I even considered completing a sub-aqua diving course with a view to visiting the site of the wreck. It was not until I decided to write an article commemorating the 50th anniversary of the ship's foundering that my interest, originally factual and clinical, became more emotional and personal. This was triggered by my Internet encounter with Pedro Tomas, a Portuguese diver who had found pieces of the wreck on the seabed and wanted to know more about how the *Hildebrand* had ended its days on his country's coast.

I am grateful to him for his initial enthusiasm, which renewed mine and then increased our efforts to piece together the story. I thank him for inviting me to co-author an article in the Portuguese diving magazine *Planetad'agua*, and for his suggestion that the whole story should be written.

An article of mine about the shipwreck was published in *Sea Breezes* magazine in May 2009 and this led to Engineer, Tony McClements getting in touch with me. He was my first contact with anyone associated with the *Hildebrand*. I am very grateful that his family discouraged his initial reluctance to communicate with me, and thank Tony for his contribution and the large part he played in all our activities concerning this story.

Not only did Tony provide a great deal of information, but it was because of this connection that the divers Pedro Tomas and Pedro Carvalho visited us in Britain. Both amateur divers and cameramen, they had decided to make a film about the shipwreck, for which they interviewed us. Tony and his family have been extremely enthusiastic about delving into further details of this story, and that resulted in us both being invited to Lisbon, courtesy of the Cascais Cultural Department, to see the finished film. The trip back to where it all happened was one I had wanted to make for many years, and we experienced wonderful hospitality from the two divers and their families, as well as Fernanda Costa and Adelaide Palet, staff of the Forte St Jorge at Oitavos, and the Portuguese people.

The film itself is masterful. I am thrilled that Pedro Carvalho applied his perfectionism and creative eye to the making of what resulted in a wonderful tribute to the *Hildebrand*, which took many hours of filming, editing, recording and money to produce. Together with Pedro Tomas, he and his family have since become my firm friends, for which I feel particularly privileged.

The story would have been told in much less detail if it had not been for the anecdotes, eyewitness accounts and photographs from various people who responded to a request published in the Daily Mail for any information about the vessel.

My thanks go to some passengers who were on board at the time or who had travelled on Booth Line ships previously: Francis Austin and Jude Thurlow who were Seminarians travelling to Lisbon in 1957 and provided much interesting information and newspaper cuttings; John Harman, who knew Roger Poultney, a passenger, and chased up news and photographs of him; Peter Hilton, who travelled on the ship many times, as did Joan Mawdsley, who arranged for unique monochrome photographs to be sent to me; and Stan Porter. Hazel

Davies sent photographs and anecdotes concerning her parents, Reg and Jess Byrne, who were on board; and Gwyneth McLoughlin and I reminisced about our times as children on the Booth Line ships. I am also grateful to Eric Cowell who provided information about passenger Elwyn Iton.

The only eyewitness account from shore came from Pat Potier who vividly described the accident from her unique viewpoint on land, and sent the only known photograph of the ship heading directly towards the coast. It was a great pleasure to meet the brothers Antonio and Carlos Guerra, who gave me the evocative photograph taken by their father showing them as children, looking at the grounded ship. It is one I shall treasure.

Information received from crew members, employees of the Booth Line and others associated with the ship was especially pleasing. Harry Baker, Able Seaman, sent numerous newspaper cuttings and other treasured personal memorabilia; Brian Balshaw told of his work as a stevedore; Debbie Gilbert-Long sent photographs of her father, an officer; Graham Evans, the Assistant Purser, provided charming anecdotes and a personal photograph in which the Captain features. I am grateful to Mrs. Harrison, whose husband worked for the Line, for the story of the ice-cream; to Frank Jones, a waiter, for his memories and photographs; to Angus Snow for his story of the cat; and to Fred Littler, Jim Rimmer, Brian Williams and Gordon Robinson (nephew of Captain Williams) for their contributions.

It was particularly exciting to hear from crew members who were on duty on the *Hildebrand* at the time of its grounding. Engineers George Clark and John Gillen provided a great deal of useful and unique first-hand information on activity in the engine room; thanks also to Engineer George Watson for his contribution; Able Seamen Frank O'Hara and Philip Astley related the incident and painted a picture of the days on board during salvage operations. I am especially grateful to Able Seaman Roger Astley, who wrote at length about the whole incident and sent me remarkable photographs. All through the process he has shown great enthusiasm for this project, becoming so caught up in his memories that he even found himself dreaming he was still aboard, dressed in his life jacket! Roger, you have added much to this story.

My thanks also go to all those friends who have encouraged the writing of this book and shown interest in the process, particularly June Lockyer who showed such fascination with the tale from the beginning; Pam Harding who has wholeheartedly supported my efforts at every stage; Wallace Trickett, who sold me his oil painting of the ship and put me in touch with Pedro Tomas; Lt. Cdr. J.M. Larby R.N. (retd), who advised me on maritime issues; Capt. R. Emtage for his interest; Gordon Rhodes who suggested I write to the *Daily Mail* for contacts; and Monica Porter and Gill Whitley of the *Daily Mail* who dealt with the responses.

Thanks are due to the Portuguese newspapers, *Diario de Noticias* of 26 September 1957 and *Diario Popular* of 25 September 1957, for photographs of the Captain, the ship in distress and the rescue operation.

I have endeavoured to obtain permission to publish photographs of the *Hildebrand* from owners of the copyright without success. It seems that over the years, due to sales of the Booth Line as well as the dispersion of documents during transfers of various departments of the Liverpool museums, details of who owns the copyright have been lost. I would be happy to acknowledge their ownership if this becomes known.

I am grateful to Tony Russell who gave me an encouraging critical analysis and edited this work. Lastly, my thanks are due to Mick Candler of Azimuth Print Ltd and to Sonia St.John who advised me about various publication requirements which helped me prepare this work for printing.

Ruthie Lockyer November 2013

THE KNOWN CREW

CAPTAIN:	Thomas Edward Williams
1st OFFICER:	Henry John Jones
2nd OFFICER (Snr.):	Horace (Harry) Goulden
2nd OFFICER (Jnr.):	James Patrick McClelland
3rd OFFICER:	Trevor Fletcher Hopper
BOATSWAIN:	Tom Manville
RADIO OFFICER:	David Beattie H. Douglas
ABLE-BODIED SEAMEN:	"Yank" McGowan, Peter Nield, Robert Roberts, Frank O'Hara, Philip Astley, Harry Baker, Roger Astley
CARPENTER:	David Evans
CHIEF ENGINEER:	Jacky Lowe
2nd ENGINEER:	Phillip Francis Wall
3rd ENGINEER:	Gough
4th ENGINEER:	George (Bill) Clark
ELECTRICAL ENGINEERS:	George Watson, James Swann
Jnr. ENGINEERS:	Dick Forbes, John Gillen, Barney Morrisey, Anthony McClements
ASSISTANT PURSER:	Graham Evans
BARMAN:	Edward (Ted) Sankey
WAITER:	Frank Jones
STEWARDESS:	Ann Carley

LIST OF PASSENGERS

FIRST CLASS

Mr. H.F. ALLEN..	Round Voyage
Mrs. H.F. ALLEN	Round Voyage
Mr. E.L. ALVES..	Trinidad
Mr. S.R. BALDWIN ..	Trinidad
Mrs. S.R. BALDWIN	Trinidad
Mrs. R. BATES	Round Voyage
Mr. A.D. BENTLEY ..	Trinidad
Mrs. A.D. BENTLEY	Trinidad
Master C.D. BENTLEY	Trinidad
Mr. J.J.W. BUCKLEY	Round Voyage
Miss M.W. BUCKLEY	Round Voyage
Mr. R.W.C. BYRNE ..	Barbados
Mrs. R.W.C.BYRNE..	Barbados
Mrs. J.M. CLARKE..	Barbados
Mrs. M.K. DEYALSINGH	Trinidad
Miss V.M.I. DEYALSINGH	Trinidad
Miss S.K.N. DEYALSINGH	Trinidad
Mr. W.N. FOSTER ..	Trinidad
Mrs. J.M. FOULDS ..	Lisbon
Mr. R.E. GARNER ..	Trinidad
Mrs. R.E. GARNER..	Trinidad
Miss M.V. GRANT ..	Trinidad
Mr. D.P. GREAVES ..	Trinidad
Mr. L.L. HEATH	Trinidad
Mrs. L.L. HEATH	Trinidad
Master G.J. HEATH..	Trinidad
Mrs. J.M. HUTTON ..	Trinidad
Mr. E.F. ITON	Trinidad
Mrs. E.F. ITON	Trinidad
Miss R.A. ITON	Trinidad
Mr. D.W. JONES	Trinidad
Mrs. D.W. JONES ..	Trinidad
Miss J.P.F. JONES. ..	Trinidad

Master A.D.F. JONES	..	..	..	..	.. Trinidad
MasterP.D.F. JONES	..	..	..	..	.. Trinidad
Mrs. I.E.M. KERNAHAN	..	..	..	..	.. Trinidad
Mr. J.C. MACNAB ..	..	..	..	..	Round Voyage
Mr. G.V. MANCINI ..	..	..	..	..	.. Trinidad
Mrs. G.V. MANCINI ..	..	..	..	..	.. Trinidad
Mr. A.E. MARSHALL	..	..	..	..	.. Trinidad
Mrs. A.E. MARSHALL	..	..	..	..	.. Trinidad
Mr. C. MILNE ..	..	..	..	..	.. Trinidad
Mrs. C. MILNE ..	..	..	..	..	.. Trinidad
Mr. W. NEVILLE ..	..	..	..	..	.. Barbados
Mrs. F.B. ODDY ..	..	..	..	..	Round Voyage
Mr. T.J. O'SULLIVAN	..	..	..	..	.. Trinidad
Mrs. T.J. O'SULLIVAN	..	..	..	..	.. Trinidad
Miss P.M. O'SULLIVAN	..	..	..	..	.. Trinidad
Master T.J. O'SULLIVAN	..	..	..	..	.. Trinidad
Mr. K.W. POULTNEY	..	..	..	..	.. Barbados
Mr. A. SMITH ..	..	..	..	..	.. Trinidad
Mr. W. THOMPSON	..	..	..	..	.. Barbados
Mrs. W. THOMPSON	..	..	..	..	.. Barbados
Miss S.P. THOMPSON	..	..	..	..	.. Barbados
Mr. D.J. De VERTEUIL	..	..	..	..	.. Trinidad
Mrs. D.J. De VERTEUIL	..	..	..	..	.. Trinidad

TOURIST CLASS

Miss R.A. ALLEYNE	..	..	..	..	.. Barbados
Mr. F. AUSTIN ..	..	..	..	..	.. Lisbon
Mrs. E. BAKSH ..	..	..	..	..	.. Trinidad
Miss C. BARRATT ..	..	..	..	..	.. Trinidad
Miss L.V. BARROW..	..	..	..	..	.. Barbados
Mrs. H. BARROW ..	..	..	..	..	.. Trinidad
Miss G.O. BARROW	..	..	..	..	.. Trinidad
Master D.M. BASANTA	..	..	..	..	.. Trinidad

Mr. N.H. BIRD	..	...	..	..	..	Trinidad
Mr. G. BURKE	..	..	..	..	..	Lisbon
Mr. P.R. CARMICHAEL	..	..	..	..	..	Trinidad
Miss A.R.M. CLARKE	..	..	..	..	..	Barbados
Miss R.R. COLE	..	..	..	..	..	Barbados
Mrs. R. CREVELLE..	..	..	..	..	..	Trinidad
Mr. G. DAVIS	..	..	..	..	..	Lisbon
Mr. C.C. DEPEIAZA	..	..	..	..	..	Barbados
Dr. LOIS E. DOUGLAS	..	..	..	..	..	Barbados
Mr. N.O. EUSTACE..	..	..	..	..	..	Trinidad
Mr. A.A. EZECHIELS	..	..	..	..	..	Trinidad
Mrs. A.A. EZECHIELS	..	..	..	..	..	Trinidad
Mr. J. FINNIGAN	..	..	..	..	..	Lisbon
Mr. B.A. FUNNELL..	..	..	..	..	..	Lisbon
Mr. P.R. GIBBS	..	..	..	..	..	Barbados
Mrs. S.C. GILL	..	..	..	..	..	Barbados
Mr. G.L. HINDS	..	..	..	..	..	Barbados
Mrs. G.L. HINDS	..	..	..	..	..	Barbados
Master R.A. HINDS..	..	..	..	..	..	Barbados
Mr. H.E. HINDS	..	..	..	..	..	Trinidad
Mr. O. HINKSON	..	..	..	..	..	Barbados
Mr. P.W. HOPEWELL	..	..	..	..	..	Lisbon
Mr. E.F. HOWARD	..	..	..	..	..	Trinidad
Mrs. E.F. HOWARD..	..	..	..	..	..	Trinidad
Mrs. E.R. HOWARD	..	..	..	..	..	Trinidad
Miss K. HUSBANDS	..	..	..	..	..	Barbados
Mrs. S.D. HUTCHINSON	..	..	..	..	..	Barbados
Miss K.A. HUTCHINSON	..	..	..	..	..	Barbados
Miss H.A. INNISS	..	..	..	..	..	Barbados
Mrs. G. JAMES	..	..	..	..	..	Barbados
Master T. JAMES	..	..	..	..	..	Barbados
Mr. P.W. JOHNSON..	..	..	..	..	..	Lisbon
Mr. A.R. JULUMSINGH	..	..	..	..	..	Trinidad
Mrs. A.R. JULUMSINGH	..	..	..	..	..	Trinidad
Miss M.S. JULUMSINGGH	..	..	..	..	..	Trinidad
Mr. J. KEEFE	..	..	..	..	..	Lisbon
Mr. N. KHAIRULE	..	..	..	..	..	Trinidad

Miss W. LAKHAN ..	..	..	..	..	..	Trinidad
Miss G.Y. LALGEE ..	..	..	..	..	..	Trinidad
Mrs. D. LARDY ..	..	..	..	..	..	Trinidad
Miss M.R. LINTON ..	..	..	..	..	..	Barbados
Rev. J.K. LOCKYER	..	..	..	..	..	Barbados
Mrs. J.K. LOCKYER	..	..	..	..	..	Barbados
Miss R.B. LOCKYER	..	..	..	..	..	Barbados
Mr. R.S. LOPES ..	..	..	..	..	..	Trinidad
Mr.W.J. McBRIEN ..	..	..	..	..	..	Barbados
Rev. J.R. MADDRAN	..	..	..	..	..	Barbados
Mrs. J.R. MADDRAN	..	..	..	..	..	Barbados
Mrs. J.J. MEYER ..	..	..	..	..	..	Trinidad
Miss C.E. MEYER ..	..	..	..	..	..	Trinidad
Mr. P. MEYER ..	..	..	..	..	..	Trinidad
Miss C.E. MILLER ..	..	..	..	..	..	Barbados
Dr. H.V. MORRIS ..	..	..	..	..	..	Barbados
Mrs. H.V. MORRIS ..	..	..	..	..	..	Barbados
Master D.V. MORRIS	..	..	..	..	..	Barbados
Master R.D.T. MORRIS	..	..	..	..	..	Barbados
Mr. P.R. MURPHY ..	..	..	..	..	..	Lisbon
Mr. W.C. MURRAY ..	..	..	..	..	..	Trinidad
Mr. J.V. NAMSOO ..	..	..	..	..	..	Trinidad
Mrs. J.V. NAMSOO ..	..	..	..	..	..	Trinidad
Mr. J.R. NEEDHAM..	..	..	..	..	..	Barbados
Mr. J.R. NOLAN ..	..	..	..	..	..	Lisbon
Mr. B.S. O'BRIEN ..	..	..	..	..	..	Lisbon
Master R.R. OJAHMAHARAJ ..	..	..	..	..	..	Trinidad
Mr. M.M. PATEL ..	..	..	..	..	..	Barbados
Mr. J. PERSAD ..	..	..	..	..	..	Trinidad
Mrs. J. PEERSAD ..	..	..	..	..	..	Trinidad
Mr. D.B. PETER ..	..	..	..	..	..	Trinidad
Miss S.K. POWER ..	..	..	..	..	..	Trinidad
Mr. W. POWER ..	..	..	..	..	..	Lisbon
Mr. R.S. QUINTON ..	..	..	..	..	..	Lisbon
Miss G.G. RICHARDS	..	..	..	..	..	Trinidad
Mr. C.H. ROLLINGS	..	..	..	..	..	Trinidad
Miss G.E. ROLLOCK	..	..	..	..	..	Barbados
Mr. T. SHEPHERD ..	..	..	..	..	..	Lisbon
Miss L. SIMMONS ..	..	..	..	..	..	Trinidad
Miss E.L. SIMPSON	..	..	..	..	..	Trinidad
Miss O.M. SNOW ..	..	..	..	..	..	Barbados

Mr. G.R. STONE	Trinidad
Mrs. G.R. STONE	Trinidad
Mr. G.H. THEWLIS	Trinidad
Mr. E.T. THORPE	Barbados
Mr. A.J. THURLOW	Lisbon
Mr. P. TIERNEY	Lisbon
Mr. C.D. TIKASINGH	Trinidad
Mrs. C.D. TIKASINGH	Trinidad
Miss B.S. TIKASINGH	Trinidad
Mr. J.F.P. TIMMINS	Lisbon
Rev. R.G. WAKEFIELD	Trinidad
Mrs. R.G. WAKEFIELD	Trinidad
Miss E.C. WAKEFIELD	Trinidad
Miss A.M. WELLARD	Lisbon
Mr. R.A. WHITEHEAD	Trinidad
Mrs. R.A. WHITEHEAD	Trinidad
Mr. F.H.X. WILLIAMS	Trinidad
Mr. P.A. WILSON	Lisbon
Mr. K.J. YOUNG	Trinidad
Mrs. K.J. YOUNG	Trinidad
Miss M.P. YOUNG	Barbados
Mr. W.S. YOUNG	Barbados
Mr. E.D. ZANETTI	Trinidad

Hildebrand leaving the dockside at Liverpool

CHAPTER 1

"ALL ABOARD"

For a start, the ship's baker and three crewmembers were missing. "Bad luck," they said, "to leave port on a Friday the thirteenth." They were seen leaving the ship and being collected by relatives waiting on the quayside. Unusually, it took some days to find replacements, so it was Saturday, 21 September 1957, at 22.30 hours that the Booth Line's one-funnelled steamship RMS *Hildebrand III* weighed anchor. With tugboats helping, she very slowly nosed her way out of the Queen's Dock at the Liverpool port to the sound of tug and ship sirens and the megaphone calls of dock officials. She was thus towed out into the blackness and the murky waters of the River Mersey.

My father, mother and I - then eight years of age - had boarded early that evening, on a typically grey, drizzly English autumn day. As darkness fell over the city, we made our way to the Customs House, where we had our passports examined and our baggage checked. This included our teachests with "MMS" (Methodist

Missionary Society) marked in big letters. As I sat on one of the boxes outside the large warehouse, we noticed some passengers were being asked to open up their belongings for inspection. My mother was dreading being ordered to do so. She need not have worried.

Hildebrand III in Queen's Dock

Also about to board were 14 men bound for the English Roman Catholic Seminary in Lisbon. As some previous students had only been twelve years of age, the college (founded in 1630) was affectionately known as *O Colegio dos Inglesinhos* ("The College of Little Englishmen"). The training for the priesthood was six years and, of the 14, four were returning from leave after three years, while the rest were embarking on their training. As their baggage was loaded, the dockers joked

2

with them: "This boat will never get there!"

Making his first journey as an officer on the *Hildebrand* was Junior Engineer Tony McClements. Just before setting sail, he lost his wallet containing all his money, which was never returned. "I felt it to be a bad omen," he said.

We were duly allowed to make our way along the gangway, welcomed aboard by the Assistant Purser, who was also making his first voyage on the ship, and guided to our cabins. These were just below deck, and being on the outside of the vessel, each had a porthole to give us a view of the sea and passing scene. Well-wishers had sent to our cabins bouquets of chrysanthemums (flowers considered by some to be a bad omen), together with their love, bidding us "God-speed" and "Bon Voyage".

Having stowed our personal baggage in the cabins, we went up on deck to see the lights of Liverpool and to watch the final preparations for departure on the decks and dockside. It was now about 7pm and soon the dinner gong sounded, so we went below to the dining room to enjoy our first meal aboard ship. This was served by an efficient Portuguese staff with whom we had some fun trying to make ourselves understood.

Afterwards, we strolled along the decks, acquainting ourselves with the ship and looking forward to the exciting adventure before us…

First class cabin

Tourist class cabin

First class dining room

Tourist class dining room

First class piano lounge

Tourist class lounge

CHAPTER 2

THE HILDEBRAND DYNASTY

The Booth Line was founded in the 1860s. It took over the Red Cross Line in 1901 and the Iquitos Steamship Company in 1911. In 1946 it was sold to the Vestey group of companies, which included the Blue Star and Lamport & Holt Lines. Lord Vestey has been described as a character. Apparently on at least one occasion he dressed up in scruffy clothes and tried to board the ship incognito but was stopped by an officer on guard who would not let him through without a pass or a ticket. Lord Vestey, normally known to be careful with his money, gave him ten shillings for doing his job!

In 1975 the entire group's ships were pooled under Blue Star Ship Management Ltd and the Booth Line ceased to exist as a separate entity.

The *RMS Hildebrand III*, in which we sailed in September 1957, was built for the Booth Line. The name Hildebrand is of Scandinavian origin, associated with mythology, meaning "one who pursues his mission, never retreating from adversity". *Hildebrand I* was constructed

5

for the German Imperial Navy in 1889, her function being coastal defence. She ran aground off the Dutch coast in 1919 and what remained of the ship was exploded in 1933.

The magnificent *Hildebrand II* was constructed in 1911 in the Greenock shipyards, in Scotland, and was a cargo and cruise liner connecting Liverpool and Brazil. She was ordered at the peak of the Brazilian rubber boom (in 1910 Brazilian production accounted for 80 per cent of the world's supply). By 1912 the rubber boom crashed due to the introduction of commercial production on British plantations in Malaya, the seeds having been smuggled out of Brazil and propagated at Kew Gardens.

During 1914-18 she was on war service and escaped attack from German U-boats. At the end of the war the Booth Line's fortunes had not improved as they faced increased competition from Lamport & Holt who had poached the Amazon trade. But between 1922 and 1930 the *Hildebrand II* was the only first-class passenger ship in the fleet whose calls included Oporto, Lisbon, Madeira, Belem do Para and Manaus. She was decommissioned in 1932 and dismantled in Monmouth in 1934.

Built by Cammell-Laird Shipbuilders in Birkenhead, the *RMS Hildebrand III*, a cargo-passenger liner, was launched on 20 July 1951, being the 1216th ship built by this famous shipbuilding empire. She was 140 meters long and was driven by two steam turbines producing 1200hp, which could propel this 7735-ton vessel to a maximum speed of 15 knots.

RMS *Hildebrand III* is launched 20 July 1951

She crossed the Mersey to a Liverpool dockside for fitting out, which was completed on 21 December, and the ship made her maiden voyage to Brazil on 28 December 1951. The *Hildebrand's* other main task was transporting cargo. She traversed the journey begun by *Hildebrand II*, but took over the route from her sister ship *RMS Hilary*, which carried tourists a thousand miles down the Amazon River to Manaus in northern Brazil by way of

Portugal, the Azores and the West Indies. In the 1920s
and '30s Manaus was famous for its large theatre, where

operas were performed with distinguished artists brought over from Europe. In the 1950s, the cruise lasted for seven weeks and

Booth Line ship arriving at Manaus

cost £75, £80 and £85 per person.

The brochure described the ship as being
"provided with every convenience for tropical travel. The
cabins, situated amidships, are for one or two
passengers. All rooms are outside ones with windows or
portholes; they are comfortably furnished and are fitted
with electric fans. The *Hildebrand* has many cabins with
private baths or showers... The public rooms comprise
Dining Saloon furnished with small tables, Lounge and
Smoking Room.

"Deck Tennis and other deck games can be played
on the Boat Deck without inconvenience to those on the
Promenade Deck desirous of rest. A swimming pool is

available on the Main Deck forward during the hot weather part of the voyage." The swimming pool was a canvas and wooden-framed contraption erected on the foredeck and filled with seawater when the conditions settled down after calling in at Madeira.

The *Hildebrand III* ran a service for almost six years between England and South America. Leaving Liverpool, she called at Oporto and Lisbon in Portugal, Madeira, and Barbados and Trinidad in the West Indies, before sailing down the Amazon to Manaus. She transported cargo, such as sugar, scrap metal and timber, across the Atlantic and provided Amazonian cruises for tourists.

During the less interesting part of the trip across the open sea, passengers could amuse themselves by

"Crossing the line" ceremony

playing ship's games, as advertised, which included golf, tennis, shuffleboard, cards and some other lighthearted games. One day was arranged for a fancy-dress event and another for the "Crossing the Line"

Tourists on Promenade deck enjoy views of life on the Amazon

ceremony as the ship crossed the equator. Once the ship had reached the Amazon, passengers could enjoy the views on the promenade deck, or even explore the creeks advertised as "Unexplored Forest".

The *Hildebrand* was a popular ship among both travellers and crew. Even while she was being built, there was a positive aura around her. An apprentice who worked for a company responsible for onboard maintenance of cargo refrigeration control equipment and of navigational aids said that he had "an exceptional fondness for the vessel – it had a nice feeling". Apparently there was competition between the sailors to work on the *Hildebrand*. One seaman described her as "a wonderful ship" having sailed on her on four occasions; another had worked on five passages and said it was his favourite ship. One of the Junior Engineers had served on nine ships with three shipping companies and a guided missile destroyer with the Royal

Navy, and considered the *Hildebrand* to be his favourite ship. Customers too reported happy memories of their journeys on the *Hildebrand*. Mrs. Mawdsley (a midwife) and her husband, a Baptist minister, worked in Brazil for 35 years and frequently travelled on Booth Line ships as her uncle was a Purser with the Line. The *Hildebrand* was their favourite.

Charles Booth 1902

It seems that the Booths were good people to work for. They were philanthropists and cared for their staff. The men earned £2 8s 0d per month, a reasonably good wage for its day. Mrs. Booth, affectionately referred to as "Maggie", would visit sick sailors in their employ.

Such was the "*Hildebrand* Dynasty", but *Hildebrand III* had perhaps the unhappiest, and certainly the shortest existence. In 1957 she was not very familiar with luck. Late on 19 April, while she was in Liverpool's Queen's Dock to unload a cargo of sugar, scrap metal and timber from South America, a fire broke out. The

Liverpool Fire Service sent four machines to assist the Port Emergency Fire Service. The local paper reported: "The outbreak was confined to a small area of planking on the main deck for'ard. The smouldering timber was quickly brought under control and the affected deck cut away. There was very little damage".

Yet all seemed well with the ship when we set off.

CHAPTER 3

"LIVERPOOL ON HER STERN, BOUND TO GO"

At the first meal on board in the tourist-class dining saloon, and afterwards on deck, we met some of the 164 passengers: people visiting emigrant relatives; rich widows on their annual holiday; newlyweds on a honeymoon cruise; West Indians having fulfilled some dream in their mother country but now homesick for their native land; and three Methodist missionaries heading for new posts in the West Indies. My father was one of the latter and as a family we were looking forward to living in Antigua in the Leeward Islands for a few years. Not only Methodist ministers and Roman Catholic seminarians, but also two Anglican clerics were sailing, members of the Muirfield Fathers, bound for the West Indies. There is a superstition that it is bad luck to have "men of the cloth" on board. If so, then with 19 clergy our journey would be decidedly precarious.

Whatever the reason for travelling, we all shared excitement about the forthcoming cruise and, at least for the Methodist missionaries, anticipation of what was in store at the journey's end.

The route was to take us from Liverpool, calling at Oporto in Portugal, then on to Lisbon to allow 17 passengers to disembark. After calling at Funchal Bay in Madeira and then crossing the Atlantic, the ship would visit Barbados and Trinidad. On this particular trip the *Hildebrand* was not taking tourists further. Disembarkation for us was to be at Barbados.

The Captain was Thomas Edward Williams, aged 53, of 12 Woodland Road, Waterloo, Liverpool who was born in that city and came from a long line of seafarers on his mother's side. Both parents were Welsh and his father was a ship's joiner and repairer. Captain Williams worked for many years with the Booth Line on the Amazon run trading in timber, Brazil nuts and rubber. Like many other officers, he trained with the Royal Navy Reserves, in which he served for the full term of hostilities in World War II. He was aboard a Booth Line vessel that was one of the first ships to be attacked off Brazil at the beginning of the war. He was awarded the DSC in 1943 after minesweeping operations in the Mediterranean, and gained the DSO because of the Dunkirk evacuation, in which he commanded the HMS *Beaumaris* and later

HMS *Speedwell*. After the war ended, he returned to the Booth Line and his previous trading with Brazil. On this voyage, he was relief Captain.

After the meal that first evening, my parents and their colleagues went up on deck again, impatient to see the vessel cast off and set sail for our far-off destinations. They were looking forward to enjoying what all hoped would be a lovely holiday cruise – the prelude to work abroad. But then she dropped anchor in the Mersey, not to sail again until next day as we waited for the arrival of the replacement baker-cum-confectioner.

Sunday morning, 22 September, dawned grey and cold. At 10.00 hours we weighed anchor again and, with its full capacity of passengers and crew and its general cargo of 2840 tons, the *Hildebrand* set off for the open sea...

The *Hildebrand* leaves Liverpool

Series I—" SUNNY SOUTH."
Published by the Booth Line, Liverpool.

A BREEZY DAY AT SEA

CHAPTER 4

"FELT UNEASY ABOUT THE SHIP"

A sunny sail down the calm Irish Sea turned to turbulence in choppy seas as evening came. There had been an unpleasant outbreak of Asian 'flu in Britain and some of the crew and passengers, including my father, had succumbed. Monday was uneventful and we sailed on looking forward to the warmer weather that we knew we would enjoy further south in the Atlantic. During the night we reached the Bay of Biscay.

The *Hildebrand*, like all the ships on this route, was built with quite a narrow draught, to enable her to travel far down the Amazon, and so in 1957, before the time of stabilisers, she was rather inclined to roll. A passenger who had travelled frequently on the Booth Line ships said that, because they were so small, "to get into a storm in mid-Atlantic was a terrifying experience." Another passenger described his first taste of sea travel on the *Hildebrand* when he crossed the Bay of Biscay in a storm. "It was so rough," he said, "the tips of the propeller were coming out of the water setting up quite a vibration in the stern."

On our crossing the Bay lived up to its reputation: we endured a terrible gale all night so we slept little. We were glad of calmer weather next day as we cruised off the coast of Spain.

On Tuesday night we arrived off Oporto on the west coast of Portugal, which was to be our first port of call. Frequently there would be a pickup here at the port, Leixoes, of some Portuguese crew. These would be for convenience of Portuguese passengers - who were often unable to understand English - who would be boarding at Lisbon to immigrate to Brazil. The Portuguese government was trying to help Portuguese nationals out of their poverty by giving them the opportunity to start new lives in another country. On previous trips one passenger noted, they generally did not seem very happy about this upheaval from their homes. As they embarked at Lisbon there would be much wailing and tears, priests praying, the using of rosary beads, and Portuguese medics performing last-minute health checks. A medical team travelled with them on each trip as well as nuns and priests, who performed Mass every morning. Although most of these immigrants were poor they have been described as "a very sociable group once we were under way in the warm seas south of Madeira... lots of fado [Portuguese songs] and dancing were performed every evening on the after deck".

Portuguese provisions and contraband for the Brazilian black market would also be loaded at Leixoes: wine, olive oil, salt cod and various kinds of cured meats. Any of these items not consumed by the Portuguese passengers would be traded and sold in Belem, in Brazil, where hundreds of Brazilians gathered at the quayside when the ship docked. The port authorities and customs officials would be first on the ship and the crowds waited for them to disappear - loaded with presents and always drunk - before they could buy goods. (Some *Hildebrand* staff were said to have made a fortune selling luxury goods in the Amazon region – it was noted that the barber who ran the ship's shop, as well as the Chief Steward, were both collected in beautiful cars when they got home again, while other crew had to use taxis and buses.) However, on this trip *Hildebrand* was only offloading 80 tons of cargo, not collecting passengers or taking on provisions because this was a shortened voyage ending at Trinidad.

Unfortunately, because of the rocky coastline and the fact that the weather had worsened, it was no longer safe to enter Leixoes harbour at Oporto, so we anchored. Soon however, further instructions were received to continue to Lisbon, so we set off again. Then down came the fog.

The bad weather and stormy seas alarmed some passengers. During the late evening Engineer McClements, on the 8pm-to-midnight watch, had to check the steering gear, which involved going along one of the passageways towards the stern. He was surprised to see a number of passengers there on their knees in prayer! There was fog for most of the night so the *Hildebrand* sounded her siren every two minutes throughout resulting in us landlubbers being unable to sleep.

Unknown to us, Captain Williams had received orders during the night to search for survivors of a 360-foot German windjammer, the *Pamir*, which had capsized 600 miles southwest of the Azores during Hurricane Carrie. The *Pamir* was a 3103-ton four-masted barque, one of the last great sailing ships, and on board were 51 teenage cadets in training for the German merchant

The MV *Pamir*

marine and 35 veteran mariners. So the *Hildebrand* had altered course as she went to the rescue, but sadly no crew were found and she returned to her original course. (Only six survivors were ever rescued from the *Pamir*. The *Times* later reported that had the windjammer been fitted with wooden masts, these would have snapped under the force of the hurricane and the boat would have righted itself. As it was, the metal masts and rigging were too strong and forced the vessel to capsize.)

Early the next morning, the *Hildebrand* began her journey, "travelling fast through thick fog" (according to Senior Engineer Bill Clark) towards Lisbon. My mother's diary entry for the morning of Sunday, 22 September reads: "Felt uneasy about the ship."

Boca do Inferno at Oitavos, near Cascais

CHAPTER 5

DOOMED!

At about 6am on Wednesday the 25th, the engineers started hearing the foghorn sounding irregularly, as if it was a warning, but this meant little to them, not being navigators. Then the Navigation Officer on the bridge sent down an order: "STOP ENGINES!" This was unusual: normally there would be a half-hour's warning first to slow down and then to stop. The engineers then heard a scraping noise alongside the ship, which, according to a Junior Engineer, "frightened the life out of us". At that time of day there would have been many fishing boats coming in after a night's fishing – in those days the coastal town of Cascais had a large fishing industry.

The crew were never keen to cruise along the coast at night because it meant that the foghorn would be employed continuously to warn fishermen. This would direct steam away from the engines, so the engineers had to work extra hard to make steam to keep the ship on a steady speed. It meant frustration in the engine room because steam generation could not be regulated to allow steady-state fuel and water consumption; the engineers had no control whatsoever. Nor were the fishermen pleased when a large ship sailed through their fishing grounds and routes back to harbour. When the engineers heard the scraping noise – "an adrenalin moment" - they believed they might have hit a fishing boat. After five or so minutes, the ship resumed her journey but the incident was not explained.

Later at breakfast in the Officers' Mess, Engineer Gillen asked Goulden, the Navigation Officer, the cause of the earlier noise. Although he did not know exactly, he said that a tug was bringing in a barge and there were men on the tug's bridge waving their fists and shouting at him. He thought they might have cut the tow rope between the two. Gillen noticed the officer was agitated about the incident: he ate his breakfast quickly and even though his watch had ended returned to the bridge.

Goulden's assessment of what happened seems to have been correct because at around this time the Second Mate on the MV *Irish Heather* described his ship as being hove to off Lisbon when they were plotting a tow heading north. Unexpectedly, they picked up a large contact inexplicably heading towards the northern entrance at Cascais, seemingly cutting across the towing and the towed vessels. The men correctly thought it was "one of Maggie Booth's" - it turned out to be the *Hildebrand*.

At some point during the early morning, it has been reported, the Captain, who had spent a long time on the bridge, and had had little sleep over the previous few nights, went to his stateroom for a rest, leaving the First Officer in charge.

Roger Astley and his brother Philip had joined the vessel as seamen but were signed on as quartermasters and set to steering the ship. That morning, Roger Astley had taken over the 8am-midday watch and at 10am was relieved for his tea break. As he left the bridge on his way down he was told to hoist the courtesy (Portuguese) flag. He noticed that the carpenter and the First Officer were already on the forecastle going about their duties ready to enter harbour. Due to the damp and foggy weather, the signal halyards were taut and it took Astley a few minutes to release them.

Meanwhile, passengers had breakfasted and many of us had gone up on deck, hoping that we would see the coast as we sailed into Lisbon. The fog was still surrounding us, but the air was warm and the brightness overhead suggested that the sun was shining gloriously higher up. Nevertheless we could not see beyond a few yards; even the sea below us, as we looked from the deck rail, was indistinct. Suddenly a woman shouted "LOOK!" We followed where she was pointing. There through a gap in the fog we saw the jagged shores of Portugal only yards away. It was from there that we had been hearing the cry of the foghorn from the Guia Lighthouse.

The Portuguese shore seen from the ship

One passenger was browsing through books in the library, which was situated on the bridge. He was rather intrigued by what he saw when he looked out of the window and, pointing, asked the Assistant Purser who managed the library, "Is this normal?" Joining him, the Officer saw breaking waves and replied with alarm, "No, it isn't!"

Astley had raised the Portuguese flag about halfway up when suddenly the ship emerged from the fog into bright sunlight. Ahead he saw cliffs and a low building like a roadhouse, later identified as a restaurant. He saw the Chief Officer on the forecastle facing the bridge and waving his arms frantically trying to draw attention, while simultaneously he saw the wheel being put over "Hard to port". One of the senior engineers said that this officer would have seen the shore before anyone else and was trying to alert the bridge, but the ship was travelling too fast to have made any avoiding manoeuvres.

That morning, Mrs. Potier, a resident of Cascais, was taking her two young children for a ride in their toy wagon along the coastal path near their home. Although it was clear out at sea, she saw there was a solid bank of fog some hundred metres from the coast. She heard a ship's hooting and then the ship suddenly appeared from the fog coming directly towards her. "I felt I wanted personally to push her away," she said. Then she saw the ship hit the rocks "with an awful crunching noise – it was a horrible experience".

One of the seminarians described his experience at that time: "The fog began to lift and we realised we were sailing head-on for the shore. We came to a halt on the rocks and then lurched from side to side, stuck."

As the ship struck the rocks, Astley had to brace himself because the heavy lifting derrick on the foremast shook and banged about from the impact, just above his head. He held on to the halyard and when the ship soon came to a stop he hoisted the flag into position. Some crew members who were in their bunks were literally thrown out of bed, including Astley's brother Philip, who was in his top bunk.

Able Seaman Baker was in his cabin and reported hearing the bottom of the ship "ripping out". Engineer Gillen had finished his breakfast and gone to visit an electrician in his cabin whom he had not seen for a while, and found that he was another victim of the Asian 'flu. Gillen stood talking to the sick man, who was leaning up in his bunk, when there was a violent noise. Although it did not throw him off his feet, Gillen thought the ship had struck a rocky shoal which he knew existed a few miles along the channel from Estoril going into Lisbon. He instinctively looked out of the porthole and saw breaking water.

My father vividly described his experience on board at that instant: "Almost simultaneously when the fog cleared, we felt a sickening, crunching, grinding noise beneath us, the ship shuddered like a town shaken by an earthquake, then lurched to starboard like a drunken thing, righted herself, then lurched to port, and holding onto deck rails, we all realised that we had been swept onto rocks. There was no panic; again the vessel righted herself and rested on an even keel (probably because, as we learned a short while after the ship struck, water was pouring into two holds and therefore weighted her down somewhat). Within a few minutes of the calamity the fog lifted altogether and the sun blazed down upon us."

Below decks, passenger Jess Byrne was doing some ironing when the ship struck. She was accompanying her husband Reg, who was going to Barbados to take up a manager's position with the Cable and Wireless Company. Although they could have travelled by air, they were on the *Hildebrand* because they did not like flying.

The Allens from Buckinghamshire, reported the ship ran aground "with a great noise" but stated there was perfect order and calm.

Meanwhile, Tony McClements, in his first appointment after qualifying as a marine engineer, was on the 8am-to-midday watch. While down in the engine room he heard a loud crunch and felt the ship shudder. Not having access to a view outside the ship, he thought we had arrived at Lisbon and that the ship had hit the dock entrance or something similar. He was filling in the engine-room log on the manouevring platform and was thrown off his feet. The Senior Engineer, Bill Clark, with him in the engine room, was almost knocked over but managed to hold on to the large manoeuvring valve wheels. From travelling half-ahead, the ship's telegraph rang down: "EMERGENCY – FULL ASTERN". To fulfil this command took time because the turbines had to slow down to halt before they could be reversed, so the ship was still moving and generating more grinding sounds as it scraped along the rocks. The telegraph kept ringing down: "STOP", then "FULL ASTERN" and "STOP" but the engineers had no time to fulfil any of these requests.

Bill Clark remembers that the ship left Liverpool late, and there had been a rough crossing through the Bay of Biscay, the Captain was speeding, trying to make up time. "I came up on deck just before my watch," said Bill Clark, "and I thought we were going far too fast for the conditions we were in." When he started his watch, he decided to make preparations for coming in to collect the pilot at Cascais and then on to Lisbon port - normally this would not be done until the bridge ordered "Standby" - but he "decided to get ahead of the game." His actions were commended at the Enquiry.

Immediately following the grounding, many of the sailors came up on deck from crew's quarters to see what was happening. Roger Astley returned to the bridge in case he was needed and heard the Chief Engineer over the tannoy reporting to the captain. Over his voice, he could hear the noise and rush of water.

The alarm bell rang in the engineers' accommodation area and within five minutes the complete engine-room crew reported for duty, engineers, donkeymen ("greasers") and firefighters. The Chief Engineer, Jacky Low, assumed command of controls, assisted by some senior engineers; two junior engineers and an electrician were told to report on deck; the rest were directed to check on obvious damage.

Junior Engineer Gillen was ordered to patrol the bottom and propeller-shaft tunnel and report back – a job he continued until six o'clock that night. First he checked the water tanks. These were double-bottomed tanks approximately 3–4 feet in height which ran along the bottom of the ship and held water for the boilers. To check the level of water in the tanks a sounding rod is placed through a sounding pipe (like a car's dipstick). He opened the cock valve on tank no. 6 starboard to insert the rod, but immediately a rush of air was released. He quickly closed the cock, and found the Chief Engineer standing beside him, eager to know the state of the tanks. He insisted that a reading should be taken and it showed that the level of the water was at least 12 inches greater than it had been at 8am, as shown by the log in the engine room. Although this did show that the tank was taking in water, Gillen tasted it anyway and confirmed that it was salty.   He tested tanks no. 5 starboard and port and found they too were holed. Also he found that the main circulating pump was not functioning properly, because a large pointed rock was interfering with the machinery from underneath.

Continuing her walk along the coastal road with her children, Mrs. Potier met a man furiously cycling towards Cascais, coming from the coastal fort, Cape Raso. As there was no telephone at the fort he was taking a message by bicycle to report the grounded ship to the Cascais authorities. She offered to let him use her telephone but he was keen to deliver the message in person.   In fact, the news had arrived before him, the alarm having been raised by the owner of the "Monte Mar" restaurant along the coast, the building Astley had spotted as he was raising the flag.

The ship slewed to starboard parallel to the cliffs and this movement broke her back. At this point, water began entering the engine room through its plates, coming in from the ship's bottom.

"Some of the standpipes used for sounding the tanks were gushing water, spurting up into the engine room", reported Senior Engineer Bill Clark, "so we knew the bottom of the ship had gone and we were open to the sea." The bridge rang down to tell the engineers there that the ship was nestled on rocks. Bill Clark replied that there was no cooling water which meant that the ship's main engines were out of action.

Captain Williams and Chief Officers quickly assessed the situation: we were well and truly stranded and helpless on rocks, so it was imperative that everyone abandon ship. The crew were ordered to swing out the lifeboats, while the Assistant Purser duly made an announcement over the tannoy: "All passengers will prepare to leave the ship. Boat stations everyone please." My parents had laughed when we had lifeboat

My father and me in lifejackets   Other passengers await rescue

drill on our first day at sea, a drill that appeared chaotic to one officer, as the crew had no idea what they were supposed to do, but this was the real thing and to the adults it sounded grim. My father collected lifebelts from our cabins for himself, my mother and me and we went to our boat stations, while the crew swung the lifeboats out on their davits to embarkation-deck level. But now the weight of the sea was causing the ship to lurch again, and a heavy list to starboard made it impossible to lower the lifeboats.

Lifeboat made ready

Jude Thurlow, one of the trainee priests, said, "At first, everyone thought it was a joke until the captain told us to get our lifejackets and then we felt a mixture of fear and excitement... as there was a group of us, we managed to have a laugh". He remembers there being panic, especially among some West Indian women who were running to their cabins screaming. Thurlow and his colleagues kept together and were talking to a single woman, who was going to Portugal to advance her career and linguistic skills, and protecting her from the unwelcome attention of one of two Test cricketers who were on board.

One of the crew confirmed that some passengers panicked, and amid the initial chaos he saw some of the crew stealing from the shop. He also noticed the Captain on the bridge with his head in his hands.

The ship shuddered with each movement so it was too hazardous to lower the lifeboats full of people and risk spilling them into the sea. Another way to disembark was needed. At one point, my father advised me to come away from the deck rails, and he described me as having to "climb up the deck" to his side.

The passengers waited on board, watching the growing crowds gathering on shore, including the Cascais fire engine which I remember my mother pointing out to me. The ship had come to rest on rocks opposite Fort St Jorge at Oitavos three miles from the fishing village of Cascais and fifteen miles from Lisbon.

"There were firefighters up there on the rocks, the port captain, those were the first people to arrive there," stated eyewitness José Luís Parracho. Also one of the first people to get to Oitavos was his father, who just six weeks later, painted a vivid picture of the ship on the rocks surrounded by tugboats.

Passengers were told not to return to their cabins, fearing that the lurching of the ship could cause doors to

People gather on shore to watch the rescue

close, which might then be difficult to open. However, my father risked it and made "one or two hurried trips" to pick up a few items including a small case, his wallet, camera and my teddy bear.

Nearing lunchtime the cook managed to provide hot soup and sandwiches for us all, though seawater was now entering the galley. "The ship's company acted magnificently, taking every care of passengers," wrote my father.

Eventually the Lisbon lifeboat and Lisbon pilot boat arrived, followed by numerous craft brought by local Portuguese fishermen and harbour workers, all keen to earn a little money by ferrying marooned passengers and crew to harbour. A gangway was lowered, and in true British naval tradition the women and children left first. Roger Astley was one of the staff assisting at the gangway, helping passengers off and making sure nobody took any baggage — even umbrellas, which the West Indian women were keen to take with them. But there was a young man who had false legs. There was quite a furore concerning his legs being offloaded with him and they were sent in a following boat, to be reunited with him shoreside. I remember seeing this disabled man amongst the crowds on deck, and wondering, with a child's curiosity, how they would manage to offload a wheelchair from the ship.

As my mother and I were about to descend, a woman asked my mother if she would take care of her three children because she refused to leave her husband. So the five of us, among others, made our way to the bottom of the gangway, where we stepped onto a fishing boat that, in my memory, seemed no more than a raft. It had a post at each corner and across the overhead beams hung grapevines bearing huge bunches of green grapes. The men had been drinking, and because of the circumstances, as well as a previous incident involving a drunken man, my mother was extremely nervous of them. The women, children and elderly who were taken on the pilot boat were given food, tea and fruit.

It seems that the Lisbon lifeboat was unable to manoeuvre alongside the ship because of the treacherous rocks of the *Boca do Inferno* ("Hell's Mouth") where the sea roars inland, in which the *Hildebrand* was firmly wedged at the mouth of the Tagus river.

As we moved away from the ship, I looked up at the huge wall of steel and saw my father at the railings. "Wave to Daddy!" ordered my mother. Recently, I found some thoughts my father had written: "I personally shall never forget, nor could I possibly describe, the emotions that I experienced as I looked down from the liner's deck rail to wave goodbye to my own wife and little daughter."

The "raft" took us to a fisherman's trawler, which then took us the three miles to the harbour at Cascais. The drama did not end there. There were a number of these boats ferrying people, and there was pandemonium around the disembarkation area. Another boat collided with ours and a woman screamed when she was almost knocked into the sea.

Jose Parracho was playing football on the beach with a friend when they heard the buzzer. "We ran to Cape Raso to see the stranded ship. There was confusion with people leaving the boat, being carried on

Fishing boats rescue passengers

fishermen's trawlers: the *Olho Marinho*, [one owned by] my cousin Agostinho and, if I remember well, the *Desejado*. And it was also the *Monte D'Ouro* or *Manelito*. There were a lot of trawlers helping out."

One of the other boats was a repository for all the suitcases and bags collected from the cabins. My mother spotted my father's blue-and-white holdall that contained all his sermons, which, being the result of much work, he always kept separate from other luggage. Not thinking of her balance or that of our boat, she stood up, pointed and shouted, "John's sermons!" A sailor, not understanding the language, held up the bag with a questioning look.

42

Fishing boat carrying luggage

"Yes!" shouted Mother frantically. He threw the bag. It was a good effort and splashed in the sea just beside us, soaking everyone around, and was retrieved before it sank. Not as fortunate was a professor at the seminary in Lisbon, who had asked one of the trainees to carry a box of his lecture notes for him. When he found that they had been lost, it was said that he nearly had a fit.

While the male passengers were still on board, the local Fire Service (the *Bombeiros Voluntarios*) made ready to fire lifelines across to the ship if there should be a need to retrieve passengers individually by breeches buoy. Fortunately, this was not necessary.

At the harbour we had to wait for a while in the fishing boats for customs officials to arrive by train from

Lisbon. One British newspaper reported that while we passengers waited for rescue, "Some sang hymns, some calypsos". (The last sentence of the report added, in the terminology of the time "Many of her tourist-class passengers are coloured." One wonders whether, even half a century ago, readers were much concerned about skin colour.) Apparently, passengers in one of the boats became restless waiting to go ashore and began a chorus of "Why are we waiting?" which is sung to the tune "Adeste Fideles" (the Christmas carol 'O Come All Ye Faithful'). In a report in a Portuguese newspaper, the song was assumed to be a hymn. The description of the event was dramatic and flowery: "The sky made an immense cathedral over the waters, and the survivors intoned hymns of praise to God. For many, their hearts filled with gratitude... and hearts of many races joined their brothers in the same fervour."

Crowds had also gathered at Cascais harbour. As we walked up the slipway, I remember a woman in a headscarf with tears in her eyes, looking pityingly at me clutching my teddy bear, murmuring "Aaah!" Her reaction surprised me because, not realising the danger, I had been enjoying the adventure.

The Mayor of Cascais met the passengers at the pier and offered us the village's hospitality. We were escorted to the Cascais Naval Yacht Club where food and milk for children was available and food ordered for the other passengers.

Eventually the 56 first-class and the 108 tourist-class passengers (the eldest, an 86-year-old woman) were taken off the ship. "Most carried handbags only, some forgot their passports," the papers reported, "but all were landed at Cascais unhurt."

My father was the last passenger to leave the *Hildebrand*, which continued to lurch violently. Bottles and tumblers from the bar shelves had continued to be scattered across the saloon floor keeping stewards busy sweeping up the broken glass, and serving sodas to all who desired them.

"I watched the whole drama," my father wrote, "and marvelled at man's resourcefulness in the midst of great emergency, and also at the British humour that many of us shared together even though every one of us found the experience most unnerving to say the least". Eventually my father also sailed away on a small boat, leaving the liner a pathetic and yet majestic sight at the mercy of the sea.

Meanwhile, down in the engine room there was much activity. The engineers spent many hours on damage reports and Gillen patrolled the propeller-shaft tunnel, which ran from the engine room to the stern. The stern was not double-bottomed like the water tanks, and he found that the tunnel shaft was also holed. A few hours after the grounding, he reported that the stern was now taking in water and he was ordered to monitor this regularly. Wisely, he decided to make certain of his escape route (a ladder up to an escape hatch) in case the watertight door from the engine room into the tunnel was suddenly closed. As it happened, Engineer McClements had found that this watertight door, which had worked perfectly during test runs, was jammed.

After a while life below became more hazardous and the crew other than the essential electricians and engineers were ordered to abandon ship. Gillen remembers that someone arrived with welcome refreshments, which were consumed rapidly, and then things worsened. The huge rolled steel joists (RSJs), or H-beams, which supported the decks and heavy machinery in the engine room, began to buckle, and the high-pressure steam pipes were being seriously stressed. Water was now entering the engine room like a fountain through the steel plates, a rock even appeared through the bottom plates, so McClements was ordered to start as many of the pumps as possible to pump water out. (Many of them were able to function because they were electrical rather than diesel pumps.) As he opened an inlet valve on the first pump, a jet of cold water soaked him - the pump had apparently fractured. Water was now coming in much faster than it could be pumped out. The Chief Engineer decided enough was enough and ordered the men to make everything safe.

"We had shut all the generators down bar one," said Senior Engineer Bill Clark. "I went up to get the pressure off the two boilers. There was a five-hundred-pound-per-square-inch pressure on them so we had to get the pressure off." As the boilers were blown down to zero pressure they vented plumes of steam from the funnels. If cold seawater had come into contact with them there would probably have been an explosion, so the safety valves were checked to let pressure off, and fans were left on to cool them. The highest generator was left running and then, as instructed, those in the engine room left their duties. The Chief Engineer told them that passengers were being taken to shore on lifeboats lowered on the non-listing side of the ship. Clark was the last man to leave the engine room, at around 10.30am, when the water was then up to his waist. He carried the engine log in a plastic bag to keep it dry.

The engineers went to collect personal belongings from their cabins but the companionways were already half full of water and only a limited amount of clothing could be salvaged; they then made ready to abandon ship. When up on deck, these men were surprised to find the Chief Engineer had left instructions that those who had collected only a small carrier bag of personal belongings were to "take care of his golf clubs", thus ensuring *his* valuables made it to shore!

Reflecting on his experience, Clark admitted, "I suppose it was a terrifying experience, but we were all too busy doing what we were trained to do... the trained deck staff had a job to do too and everyone seemed to be doing it and we didn't feel any sense of panic."

While waiting to disembark, Gillen and Clark discussed the possibility of having to swim to shore. "I doubt whether we would have been able to," said Gillen, "but we *did* talk about it. Actually, our rescue was quite scary," he added. "Our rescue craft was a very small fishing boat with a very grizzled skipper who had to creep right to our gangway, dodging rocks and having to cope with the Atlantic swell and breaking waves." The skipper had a crew of three, all of whom were his sons, aged between 14 and 18 years. There was a shrine behind the small wheelhouse with a lighted candle to *Nossa Senhora do Fatima* (Our Lady of Fatima) - a title given to the Blessed Virgin Mary because she appeared as an apparition to three shepherd children in 1917 at Fatima, Portugal. Given that the few *Hildebrand* crew had to jump onto this craft in these conditions, Gillen felt the shrine "seemed like a good idea!" From enquiries in broken English and Portuguese, Gillen discovered that there were no lifejackets for the skipper and his sons, so as they came into harbour, he and the others left theirs for them. Other lifejackets were piled up at the quay where previous passengers and other crew members had landed and had discarded them.

"During the whole incident," reported Gillen, "I saw anxiety, stress and worry but no panic, no falling out, no senior engineers 'cracking up'. Everyone did what they had to do without rancour and we were all safe."

Most of the seamen had been taken to Lisbon during the late afternoon, but it was dark when the last officers landed and were taken by bus to the Hotel Casa de Torres in the Belem district of Lisbon. The hotel was named after the famous Tower of Belem on the bank of the River Tagus – a monument to Portuguese adventurers.

The next morning they told the shipping agent who visited them that they had no money... which wasn't entirely true. So the agent arranged with the hotel that he would take care of their beer bill, but next day they were limited to six beers each. "I think the first day's beer bill must have shocked him!" said Gillen.

By evening, 84 of the crew had been taken off, leaving aboard the Captain, reported by Booth Line to be "one of their most experienced captains", and 12 other crew members.

The trainee priests were eventually taken by bus to their college at ten o'clock that night. They immediately sent telegrams home to their families back in Britain who had heard of the accident on the BBC one o'clock news. It had been a long wait for them to hear that their loved ones were safe.

Back home in Liverpool a dog sensed that all was not well. His name was Rex, the beloved spaniel of Engineer McClements, with whom he had grown up and formed a close bond. That Wednesday evening Rex, who was never allowed up the stairs in the family home, unusually went upstairs and sat whining outside his owner's bedroom. McClements' parents tried to coerce him downstairs but he refused and spent the entire night there whimpering. What was happening to his absent master?

Site of former slipway at Cascais harbour with Yacht club.
The harbour has been redesigned since 1957.

CHAPTER 6

CHEAP DAYS OUT IN LISBON

Some passengers and crew spent the night in Cascais and some in nearby Estoril, but most, including my family, stayed in the beautiful capital of Lisbon, where we would remain for five days before resuming our journey. We were accommodated in the Hotel Borges in Rua Garrett, which is situated fairly centrally. A small camp bed had been put into one of the rooms so that all the Lockyers could be together. From the bedroom window we had a view of life in the city, and I remember my mother calling me to see a woman pass by wearing a hat with a huge brim in which were tiny, fluffy, *live* yellow chickens – presumably she was off to the market.

One evening, my father ordered a grapefruit juice. The room-service porter brought him a glass of thick maroon-coloured juice which was discovered to be made from crushed red grapes. He ate and drank it anyway. Such are the relatively trivial memories that stay in a child's mind.

The Booth Line's agents visited all passengers to

make sure we were comfortable. One woman's children aged three and seven were sick with Asian 'flu and, she said, "the Booth Line sent a doctor from the British hospital to attend them and supplied medicine and attention free of cost. He even rang up the next day to find out how the children were."

Meanwhile, Superintendent Peter Thompson was dispatched from London to oversee the event and its rescue operation. His first message to the owners in London read "Send golf clubs," which indicated that the loss was serious or total.

The day after we left the ship, we visited the British Embassy. Not knowing any Portuguese, we found getting there difficult. At the Embassy there was little practical help to be had, except the "gift" of a few pounds for essentials: adults were entitled to £10 each, children £5. However, this was hardly enough for the couple with a ten-week-old baby, who needed nappies and baby food.

With the money my parents were given, my father bought the smallest book I have ever seen, still in my possession: a Lilliput Portuguese-English dictionary. He had always been interested in languages and had won the Greek prize at Richmond College in London when training, but unfortunately this little dictionary cannot have helped him a great deal because it did not have English translated into Portuguese. I am moved now when I remember that, although they had lost everything they owned, they took me shopping to buy a toy. In the shop, my father said I could buy the circus acrobat that I had picked up, a cardboard two-dimensional cutout with jointed limbs that spun the figure around when two wooden slats were squeezed together. Not wanting to deny Teddy, I bought him a fine blue dressing gown! The shipwreck was front-page news, so of course my parents also bought papers.

Each day while in Portugal, passengers made visits to the Customs House in Cascais to look for any belongings that might have been brought in from the ship. Many visits revealed that only our cabin luggage - with "many articles missing" - had been retrieved from the wreck. My mother wrote in her diary: "One of the worst days I ever remember. No clothes and no news. 5 o'clock went to Customs and there all over the floor our clothes and belongings. A terrible experience to see the faces of people who lost everything. A day I shall never forget". We were informed that all our possessions must be accounted lost – a sombre thought because that cargo included all we possessed, and it was not fully insured.

No lives were lost, but many were changed. As people searched among the items asking each other if there was anything specific they were looking for, stories began to emerge. Elwyn Iton, a Jamaican, had been returning home for a *viva voce* for his university doctorate, having studied fungal pathogens of arable crops. He had saved for many years to take his family to Britain so he could pursue postgraduate study at Cambridge, but he had registered his work with the University of the West Indies, so he had to be examined there. He was bound for Trinidad with his wife and young daughter to take up a university lectureship. Standing in the huge warehouse in what looked like a jumble sale, this tall, bearded, imposing West Indian told my father, with tears on his cheeks, that all the copies of his thesis, involving four years of work, were lost. For every survivor, the consequences of the wreck were unique and personal.

It seems odd that I, who never enjoyed reading as

a child, still have a book borrowed from the *Hildebrand's* passenger library. Perhaps there were limited activities for children on board in those days so my mother attempted to find a diversion for me. I can remember her taking me to choose a book as if it was a very grown-up thing to do. It is a most uninspiring specimen of children's literature, being a play "on the life and stories of Hans Christian Andersen" called *The Washerwoman's Child* by Alison Uttley. I guess I may have been attracted by the words "Child" and "Christian" as well as by the red cover - but I never read a word.

We busied ourselves as best we could in Lisbon. One day we took a bus along the coast to see the wreck and to take photographs. In her diary my mother notes:

"A sorry sight. By now, we were all feeling very depressed. The ship was listing more and we expected it

to go over." Over the next few months, the men from the Lisbon seminary would regularly board the coastal train to Cascais on their days off, to see the gradual deterioration of the ship.

Another day – maybe more than once – we had a tour around the capital by bus, which was extremely cheap. It became a standing joke that the cheapest entertainment on earth was a threepenny bus tour around Lisbon.

Locally, there were serious fears for the fishing and tourist industries because of oil spillage. The *Hildebrand* contained a large quantity of oil, and if she remained much longer on the rocks and if equinoctial gales damaged the oil tanks, then a further disaster might be expected.   The stranded ship was also an attraction to local people.   While the *Hildebrand* lay in Portuguese waters - sometimes, depending on the tide, in water only 24 feet deep - many divers and fishermen visited the wreck site.   A fisherman now in his early sixties remembers that the site was his "playground".

Severino Ribeiro, who was 19 at the time, said: "I was on the beach and received the news that a ship was stranded in Oitavos. We waited a few days for the sea to calm down as after the accident the sea became rough. We then went there in an outboard motor boat. There we found the fiscal guard and other officials.   The fiscal guard didn't let us see certain things, the ship was under their surveillance.   We asked their permission and went to see inside the ship. We could see the cargo holds filled with seawater, and some automobiles inside. The passenger cabins were also flooded."

Fisherman José Luís Parracho confirmed that "the ship was broken. The bottom was broken and when we were inside we could hear the sound of the water gurgling inside."

Portuguese fiscal guards and customs officials were strategically placed to guard the ship and shoreline from looters. "Whenever we needed to go there," said Parracho, "the guard was always with us, and when we were leaving the wreck we were all inspected to make sure we did not carry anything from the ship. They also checked our pockets. But I've been there only once, I never returned to the ship. I went onboard one time, to put a padlock in the bridge. I placed the padlock and left the ship. That was scary, I was afraid of that."

"Some time after the accident, objects started to appear by the shore," said Ribeiro. "There were boxes of soap, clothes… the people on the beach were all trying to get some of these items. And the fiscal guards, who were aligned along the beach, used to come after us because we weren't allowed to pick up anything that came out of the ship. But sometimes we got away with one or two items," he said with a grin. "I did pick up a few boxes of soap. I then went to do military service and I often asked my mother to give me a piece of soap for a shower while there. And she used to give me a piece or so".

Europe was still recovering from a world war and some items were scarce, or even unknown, throughout the continent. "Another thing we had by that time," said

Ribeiro, "was Ovaltine, which appeared on the shore having come from the boat. We picked that up. That was funny as we used to drink it dissolved in milk or water... as a light drink". He grinned coyly "And it was tasty, at that time it was very useful."

On Sunday, 29 September, a Booth Line agent told us that we would all be flown to our destinations in the West Indies either that night or the next (except for the cruise passengers who returned to Britain and 17 short-cruise passengers finishing their trip in Portugal). In all, 70 people were flown to their destinations in the West Indies in those two days. "It was uncomfortable, cramped and tiring – but it was no small task to produce two planes with transatlantic range at such short notice," said Mrs. O'Sullivan, a first-class passenger. Our family was told that we were to fly to Barbados the following night. My mother, who was not a nervous person normally but had never flown before, hardly slept on the Sunday night, as she was "much too afraid of the journey". She wrote: "How much can happen in a week?"

Eighty-five of the crew left for Britain, together with some salvaged baggage, in the sister ship RMS *Hubert*, which was returning from its Amazonian cruise. On board was a film crew who had been in the West Indies making the film *Island in the Sun*, starring Harry Belafonte.

One couple, passengers on the *Hildebrand* who were going to Trinidad, had not wanted to continue their journey by air as other passengers had done because they had lost a son in a 'plane crash. They waited in Lisbon for a few days and caught the *Hubert* on its return journey to the West Indies.

The next evening we left the hotel, where people had been extremely kind to us all, and boarded a 74-seater DC-4 Douglas Skymaster, a four-engine propeller, owned by American Overseas National Airways. As we took off from Lisbon Airport, my poor mother was sick with fear and tried to lift herself off the seat so as not to weigh down the aircraft! After flying all night and refuelling at Santa Maria in the Azores (4am) and Bermuda (1pm) – where I remember that the runway was parallel to the coast - we landed in Barbados at 9pm. I had been asleep when the aeroplane had flown over our final destination, Antigua, and remember being upset that one or other of my parents hadn't woken me so that I could see where I would soon be living. This was almost continuous flying – certainly we never left the aircraft – and meals were not provided at times when our stomachs indicated that they should be. My mother asked an air hostess (as they were then called) if she had anything I could eat and she managed to find a Danish pastry left over from a breakfast tray.

We stayed for a couple of nights in Bridgetown, Barbados, guests of the island's Methodist minister until Thursday, 3 October, when we boarded a British West Indies 32-seater Dakota. Finally we flew the last leg of the journey, island-hopping across St Lucia, Martinique and Guadelupe before arriving at our new home, Antigua, at 2pm. Would any of our belongings be joining us?

Some of the salvaging crew

CHAPTER 7

SALVAGE OPERATIONS AT
"A ROCK NEAR LISBON"

Once the 164 passengers and majority of the 98 crew had been rescued during the day of 25 September, a skeleton crew remained on board consisting of 14 men, six of these volunteering at the request of the Captain - "preferably single men" - including the Astley brothers and their friend Peter Nield, who were all from Blackpool. The others included officers and able seamen, the radio operator, carpenter, boatswain, donkeyman and storekeeper.

Some of the volunteers

The ship continued to sway dangerously so a pilot boat was positioned to hold the ship's stern off the rocks until tugboats arrived from Lisbon. On the afternoon tide two tugs tried to pull the ship free but failed to move her. The General Manager of the Booth Line, L. G. Deyes, expected that there would be another attempt to refloat the ship shortly before five o'clock on the following morning's tide.

By evening, the *Hildebrand's* list was reported to be dangerous. By then, two of the holds were flooded as well as the tunnel and the engine room up to 16 feet. There was "a gaping hole in her bow", which was imprisoned by rocks, and hatches 2 and 3 were also holed. One tug remained linked to the ship and two others were standing by, one each side of her. According to a maritime official "the chances of the ship being refloated were slight, as the rocks perforating the bottom had made the leaks bigger and the flooding worse." Nevertheless, a spokesman for the Booth Line said, "The ship is taking in water but we are expecting she will be able to make Lisbon harbour." That evening, the Captain warned the remaining crew that by daybreak the ship might turn over. Their first night aboard was therefore an anxious time because occasionally the ship gave an extra-hard shudder with the sea swell, and they thought, "If the worst happened, how would we get out?" There was no electricity or water because the engine room was submerged, as were their quarters, and they sat in a semicircle all night on chairs facing the double doors of the bridge.

Early the next day a company representative climbed the Jacob's ladder, making an incongruous spectacle. He was smartly dressed with a bowler hat and umbrella, looking every bit the English gentleman. He asked to see the Captain, after which the volunteers were ordered to gather anything worth salvaging, such as deck cargo and bedding and to put it in a central place.

The Assistant Purser also arrived to retrieve passengers' possessions. His job the previous day, in an office in Lisbon, had been to organise accommodation for all the passengers and crew. Now his task over the next few days would be to acquire onward transport for everyone, but for this he needed passports and other documents. Since passengers had locked their cabin doors after collecting their lifebelts and had never returned, the doors had to be forced open, which required tremendous power, with the water rising higher and higher.

The volunteers attempted to access their quarters but these were submerged, so the only clothes they had were what they were wearing. Ladies' nylon knickers were found floating about and, because these were quick-drying, some of the men used them as the only change of clothes!

After the night of sleeping on deckchairs, the volunteers were able to sleep in first-class cabins. They had to scrounge for food and they made "cheese and bully sandwiches", but when these ran out the Chief Engineer found tinned food in storage below which they cooked on portable stoves. Roger Astley added, "After a few days we got used to our surroundings and became organised. Water and food was brought out to us every day and we managed to make the generator function again." Philip Astley wrote to his mother back home in Blackpool, assuring her that he and his brother were safe, but added, "If you write back our address is: 'A rock near Lisbon'!"

One of the tasks for the men was to paint over the ship's logo on the funnel, in black, and this was done

within a couple of days. It was considered an unwanted advertisement for a ship to be seen stranded; certainly the sister ships did not need to see her in distress. However, the vessel was an obvious casualty, and was seen by numerous other ships sailing to Lisbon. Frank Jones, a waiter on the *Hubert*, remembered seeing the *Hildebrand* soon afterwards, fast on the rocks down by the head.

"It was really sad," he said, "to see the ship in such a state, with the company logo painted off her funnel." He had served on the *Hildebrand's* previous voyage. A passenger also on that trip, who had sailed on the *Hildebrand* many times, said she was so near the coast that at low tide one could have thrown a stone at her.

The following day, 26 September, tugboats, including the *Em. Z. Svitzer* and the high-powered Swedish oceangoing 527-ton tug *Herakles* arrived, having been summoned from Gibraltar, and put large generators on board to pump water out of the vessel and refloat her. Some did not approve of this strategy, thinking that the gear could drag her further on the rocks and make things worse. All portholes and hatches were tacked shut and compressed air pumped in to make the vessel more buoyant. Yet even though the weather conditions were excellent, with brilliant sunshine and calm seas, attempts to refloat her on the morning and afternoon tides were unsuccessful. For one thing, high tide on the Thursday was lower than that on the previous day, which reduced the chances of refloating her. During one of the attempts, the cables from the tugs bent the

bow guard rails. Parracho recalls, "The tugboats tried to pull her off the coast but the cables broke apart. The ship slid to another position

Salvaging crew with broken rails

Generator taken on board

and stayed there."

Other generators were supplied from shore to work cranes which were secured within the walls of Fort St Jorge. Here, the Cascais Fire Department had an important role in the rescue operation, helping to recover some cargo from the *Hildebrand* by a come-and-go system, such as was commonly used to retrieve passengers from shipwrecks close to the coast. The system was mounted on a tripod within the walls of Forte St Jorge, and a rocket was fired carrying thick steel wires, as well as instructions on how to use the system. A thinner cord was then tied to a higher point on the ship and, by means of a pulley, cargo could be transferred to shore.

Over the ensuing days the skeleton crew continued to retrieve as much of the 2840 tons of general cargo as possible. First, animals that should have been offloaded at Leixoes needed to be taken off the ship, and the Secretary of the RSPCA wanted assurance that they would be attended to. The animals, which included some pedigree pigs, were looked after by the volunteers, who supervised their removal a few days after the incident. There was also a valuable racehorse on board, which for some reason was kept in a horsebox on deck and was a favourite of some of the crew, who gave it extra food. The crew cheered as the animals were taken off.

Of course, consumables also had to be offloaded quickly. A consignment of ice-cream was dispatched back to Britain and, in the Liverpool Booth Line offices at their Friday meeting, staff were asked if anyone could use it. A man readily accepted some and took it that evening to a Boys' Brigade meeting at St Giles Church in Aintree Lane, so the young lads had an extra treat.

Other cargo was then offloaded, including 171 tons of iron, manufactured goods, machinery and cosmetics. A huge mobile crane on the aft deck was unable to be moved and prevented over 20 Land Rovers being recovered. Also on board was a consignment of 60 motorcars destined for Barbados and Trinidad, and it is rumoured that, for some years after the incident, "salvaged" vehicles were used in and around Cascais as taxis. There were also "several motor lorries, tractors and vehicle chassis." One of the trainee priests reported that a Romanian-naturalised Portuguese man bought part of this cargo and set up a temporary shed on the shore selling valuable items, like Jaguar cars - only to discover that he had to pay the (probably high) import duty.

The skeleton crew spent two weeks on board altogether, continually stepping over cables and pipes linked to the generators. They even linked up the ship's projector to a generator and, sitting on the deck, enjoyed films destined for showing to the passengers during their journey. One of them was *The Yangtse Incident*, the true story of HMS *Amethyst,* which was caught up in the Chinese Civil War in 1949 while sailing on the Yangtse River.

Each day sightseers came to watch operations from the clifftops, and at night they shone their car headlights onto them. At weekends the more affluent people arrived in their yachts with bikini-clad girls asking for "mementoes", especially with *Hildebrand* or Booth Line logos, as the

Hildebrand was a popular ship in Lisbon. Around that time many Lisbonians could be seen smoking Du Maurier cigarettes and Havana cigars...

The Captain and 12 crewmembers remained on board, but on 9 October they were forced to abandon ship, as the bow was nearly under water and "fierce waves several yards high" broke over the vessel. Philip Astley recalls, "Our last night on board the weather worsened and the sea became very rough, in fact it woke us up. On going on deck we saw waves crashing over the bridge. The fishing boat that was supposed to stand by in emergency had left with the Customs Officers."

By this time the ship was reeling hard. The shoring of the port side, erected during the first two days after the mishap, was washed away like matchsticks. The Captain thanked the men for staying on with him but told them the time had come to abandon ship. But without the fishing boat they were left to fend for themselves, so they slung a rope ladder over the side and were taken off by one of the deep-sea tugs' lifeboats. This operation took quite a while. "Seeing this bobbing about on the large waves did not inspire us to jump into it," Astley continues - their timing had to be exactly right.

Eventually they all left the ship, Able Seaman O'Hara being the last, and they stayed awake for the remainder of the night on the tugboat *Herakles* which took them to Lisbon the next morning. By daybreak the night's tempestuous seas had broken off the *Hildebrand's* rudder.

By that time, holds 1 and 5 had been emptied and the other three holds were being cleared. A Booth Line spokesman stated, "We cannot say when we shall be able to refloat her. We are getting on with the job as fast as we can." The salvage vessels made many attempts over the next few weeks to refloat the ship, but without success.

Captain Thomas E. Williams

Captain Williams was the last man to leave the ship. "Tears ran down his face as he left by launch for the shore," reported the *Liverpool Echo*. "He did not say a word, but waved to the liner as the launch left." Soon after his arrival back in Britain, Captain

Williams tendered his resignation, which was formally accepted but was not put into effect until the Enquiry was concluded. Nevertheless, whatever the results of that Enquiry might be, apparently he would not be staying with the Booth Line.

The volunteers who had remained on board with the Captain eventually returned to Britain on 19 October on board the RMS *Alcantara*. They arrived in Southampton as "Displaced British Seamen" possessing nothing more than what they wore, and were amused when asked by customs officials if they had anything to declare. As a result of their experience, they each received £60 for the loss of their uniform and were promised a job for life with the Booth Line. An able seaman stated that he was given £9 10s 0d by his union.

Given that so many of the *Hildebrand* crew lost their uniforms, it is remarkable that one Ship's Officer managed to retrieve his. Fred Littler had signed off as Radio Officer on one ship but was unexpectedly required to join MV *Roscoe* in British Guyana. He had to leave suddenly by aeroplane and have his uniform, which was being cleaned, sent on, which it was: it was in the Chief Officer's cabin on the *Hildebrand*. He was reunited with it in Trinidad some weeks later, the *Hubert* having presumably collected it in Lisbon.

On 28 October the salvage crew abandoned their task because of bad weather, and the *Hildebrand* was declared a total loss. According to the *Liverpool Echo* on 6 November virtually all the cargo had been removed, its value estimated at £1 million. The empty vessel was considered to be worth the same amount.

On 9 November, the *Birkenhead News and Advertiser* reported that the ship was breaking up. "Salvage officials who have been working on the vessel have given up hope of saving her and have accepted that wind and tide will complete the breakup which has already started."

The ship was now the property of the insurance company, which arranged for her dismantling. This was considerably helped by the pounding of heavy seas and the strong winds of the Atlantic. Fractures were now beginning to develop amidships at the bridge superstructure, and divers reported that the portside plating was holed for about 18 feet. The machinery was completely submerged and all the holds were tidal and heavily contaminated with fuel oil. This must also have affected the surrounding waters and caused damage to the local fishing and tourist industries.

At this point, another sister ship of the *Hildebrand,* the *Hilary*, was docked in Liverpool, surrounded by rumours about her future. There had been some Greek interest but negotiations had come to nothing. The stranding of the *Hildebrand* therefore suited the *Hilary* in that she could perhaps now take over the route, and in December a statement by the owners said the *Hilary* was being "diverted from another run".

Several years later, the Booth Line bought some Belgian Congo ships after the Congo became independent. One of these, the *Thysville*, replaced the *Hildebrand* and the *Hilary* to maintain the other half of the *Hubert's* route to Manaus. She was renamed the *Anselm*.

Hildebrand succumbs to rough seas

CHAPTER 8

AFTERMATH

Many months later, when we had made some semblance of a life in Antigua, we received a teachest, containing rotting linen, another teddy bear and some warped and much-stained books.

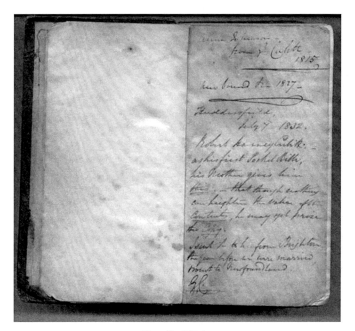

Family Bible

One of the salvaged books has quite a tale to tell. It was an 1812 family Bible originally bought in 1815 by one

Rev. George Cubitt

George Cubitt for his fiancée. He too was a Methodist minister and an ancestor of mine. After their marriage the following year, the couple went to Newfoundland as some of the first missionaries there.

Strange to relate, while in Newfoundland he too was shipwrecked. He survived, and among the few possessions that were saved was the Bible. (Back in Britain some years later, Cubitt made a name for himself as one of Methodism's great preachers and eventually became the Book Steward at the Epworth Press in London. He is buried next to John Wesley in City Road.) The Bible was passed down the generations until it reached my mother, his great-great-granddaughter. So it had been shipwrecked and salvaged again - 141 years after its first oceanic immersion. It is now in my hands. So far as our other possessions were concerned, material things had not been very important to my parents before the shipwreck, and afterwards never were again. My mother would readily give away any of her belongings without a second thought or regret.

Nevertheless, it is sad to think that only one of my mother's paintings was ever retrieved or returned to her. As a teenager in London she had attended the Slade School of Art, and she was a competent watercolourist. The only painting that survived was one she had done in 1932, at the age of fourteen, showing a lonely nighttime street corner partly lit by a lantern. She painted it one evening when she had been stood up by a date. It is a haunting piece.

Reg and Jess Byrne lost most of their possessions. Reg Byrne was particularly upset at losing his stamp collection which, he said, would be "feeding the fishes". Roger Poultney, like Reg Byrne, worked for Cable and Wireless and was travelling to his first posting abroad. He shared a rescue boat with W. Thompson and the two conversed. On reaching shore, Mr Thompson was reunited with his wife and his daughter Sheila, who had travelled together by an earlier boat, and he presumably introduced the young bachelor. Roger and Sheila then met several times in Lisbon while waiting for their onward flights, and afterwards wrote regularly. Announcing their engagement in the Cable and Wireless staff magazine *Zodiac,* a short report was headlined "Romance started on the rocks". The couple were married in April 1962. So the shipwreck did have a positive aftermath for some.

Elwyn Iton, who lost all copies of his doctoral thesis, did take up his post as a lecturer in Trinidad and rewrote his thesis on arable crops, but it took him many years.

The seminary in Lisbon tried to recoup the value of the trainee priests' belongings, but found that, under maritime law, a shipping company is not responsible for passengers' luggage. Passengers were able to insure with the ship's Purser, but this knowledge was useless after the event. So a *Hildebrand* Appeal Fund was set up by two Catholic priests, one based in Liverpool and the other the President of the English College in Lisbon. They made an appeal in the *Catholic Herald* for donations to support the seminary students who had lost all their belongings, including study books and enough clothes for three years. "The total loss to our students," they said, "is estimated at over £900. None of them can afford to lose what they have lost." By the end of the year the President wrote again, thanking contributors for having raised the full amount, and on behalf of their parents and relatives expressed "their gratitude to all who have helped to relieve them of a terrible anxiety". One of the trainee priests, Jude Thurlow, was lucky in that his mother had written on his luggage "Wanted on voyage". It seems he may have been the only passenger not to have lost any belongings since his trunk accompanied him to his cabin, much to the chagrin of his companions who therefore had less room to move about.

As for the *Hildebrand* crew, many stayed with the Booth Line. The *Hubert* was still traversing the route and a number of the now unemployed crew who had "wreck discharges" joined this ship or the *Hilary*. Gillen took extended shore leave and during that time met his wife. Luckily for McClements, one of the *Hubert's* engineers was leaving to get married, so he was able to fill the vacancy. When he returned to the same shop in Liverpool to buy his Booth Line uniform, which he had lost in the wreck, the assistant recognised him. To avoid a long explanation he told her that he was a twin brother!

A year after the incident, on 2 December 1958, the ship's back was broken by the pounding of the waves. A man was trapped on board and rescue squads were summoned to his aid. The wreckage had been bought by a Portuguese firm several months before.

The dismantling of the *Hildebrand* continued for a few years, carried out mainly by three workships, the *Espana*, the *Puenta del Burgo* and the *Luisa*. In June 1962 a tragedy struck the *Luisa*, which capsized and sank in the same place as the *Hildebrand*, with 34 tons of cargo. Happily, its crew of five escaped unharmed, but since then the retrieving of cargo from the *Hildebrand* by divers has been frustrated by problems of identifying the wreckage and the cargo's original position on the ship.

Only the *Hildebrand's* stern half remains

CHAPTER 9

THE CAT THAT CAUSED THE WRECK

Before considering the results of the Formal Enquiry, I should mention some less than serious explanations that have been offered to account for the wreck.

The superstition that it was bad luck to have "men of the cloth" aboard ship has already been mentioned. Conversely, might it have been good luck to have 19 of God's foremost servants to protect us all?

Or did the presence of a stray cat on board the *Hildebrand* have something to do with the ship's demise? In 1957 Angus Snow was Fourth Officer on the MV *Port Wyndham* in Auckland, New Zealand, which was loading cargo before heading for Britain. On the last night in Auckland a stray kitten was smuggled on board by some colleagues after a night out at a local hostelry. The next day they sailed for the South Island and the Captain noticed the kitten. As pets were not allowed on the ships, he sternly told the men to offload it before leaving New Zealand. Just before sailing, however, a blowback from a boiler started a fire in the engine room. Carbon dioxide from the ship's firefighting system and foam from the town's firefighters curbed the blaze, but the result was a mess that took ten days to clear up. Understandably, the cat was forgotten.

The *Port Wyndham* belatedly set off across the Pacific for the Panama Canal. Five days later she ran into dense fog, turbulent seas and then a hurricane. The waves were enormous and she was lucky not to founder. Eventually they passed through the eye of the storm and into calm weather, though the engines broke down no fewer than 26 times. Eventually, the *Port Wyndham* arrived through heavy seas at Port o'Spain in Trinidad.

While the ship was waiting for repairs before the final journey to Britain, the cat wandered into the Captain's stateroom. The mate was firmly reminded that the animal was to be removed from the ship. Tied up next to the *Port Wyndham* was the *Hildebrand*, and on its poop deck sat a large tom cat. A deal was struck with the *Hildebrand's* Quartermaster and the *Port Wyndham's* kitten was transferred. There were no further difficulties for the rest of the journey.

A quick turnaround saw the *Port Wyndham* sail again for Australasia. Just before arriving at Cape Town, news reached the ship of the grounding of the *Hildebrand*. Given the difficulties they had had on their previous trip while the cat was with them, and now hearing of the fate of the *Hildebrand*, the *Port Wyndham's* crew, superstitious sailors all, attributed these misfortunes to the cat. As Snow remarked, "The coincidences were too compelling!"

Officer with ship's cat

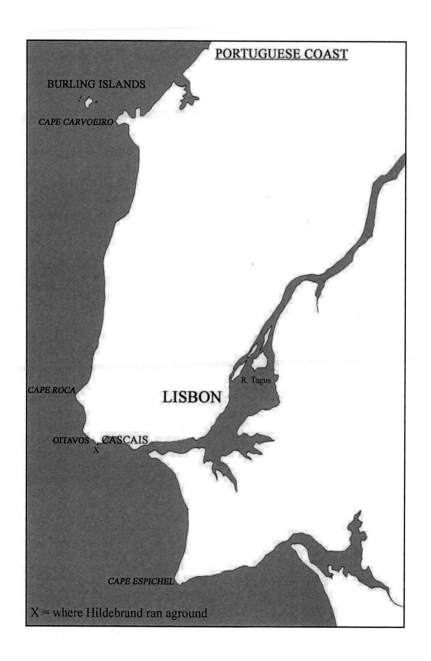

PORTUGUESE COAST

BURLING ISLANDS

CAPE CARVOEIRO

CAPE ROCA

LISBON

R. Tagus

OITAVOS   CASCAIS
X

CAPE ESPICHEL

X = where Hildebrand ran aground

CHAPTER 10

FORMAL ENQUIRY

From 3 to 5 February 1958 a Formal Investigation for the Ministry of Transport was held by the Assessors in Liverpool before Roland Adams QC, Wreck Commissioner.

There is hardly ever just a single cause of a disaster, but a series of incidents. In this case, these culminated in the Captain making errors of judgement that guided the ship onto rocks.

So what was happening on the bridge from the time the *Hildebrand* left Oporto?

The ship steamed at full speed southwards down the Portuguese coast, taking a route inside the small Burling Islands. By 6.40am on 25 September she was two miles due east of the islands and Second Officer Goulden drew a course line on the working chart. Twenty minutes later the ship came across patches of fog, so the Captain was called and took over from Goulden. "Standby" was rung down to the engine room, regulation fog signals sounded and a lookout posted on the forecastle.   From eight o'clock echo-soundings were made and depths reported at frequent intervals.

Since the ship had no radar, bearings were taken from the Radio Direction Finder. These would normally be from lighthouses at Capes Espichel and Roca but the latter was not answering. The Radio Operator admitted that much of the subsequent trouble stemmed from the fact that he was always trying to pick up Cape Roca, which proved to be useless. A substitute bearing was taken from Cape Carvoeiro many miles away near Peniche on the north coast. These were plotted on the chart at 9.20am, at which time steering was altered to a course whereby the ship headed roughly southeast, to go around the cape and along the coast eastwards towards the mouth of the Tagus at Lisbon. The Captain expected that, once they were around the cape, the fog would clear.   For the next twenty minutes, Goulden was just concerned with identifying the ship's position, not speed or course, because a bearing was now available only from Cape Espichel. During this time the ship travelled six miles and Goulden placed Cape Espichel's position at 135^0 relative to the ship. However, one of the positions, either at 9.20am or at 9.40am, must have been wrong, because the ship would not have made six miles at full speed. The true position was over a mile further seaward than plotted.

One has to sympathise with Goulden, reportedly "a very nice guy", who had been agitated that morning because of his belief that they had cut across a towed vessel and the one towing it. According to one crew member, it is reasonable to assume that he was not as focused as he might have been, and therefore made incorrect calculations.

From 9.40am onwards, the problems intensified and the Captain did not refer to the chart again. A fog signal was heard but it was not identified – was it one or two blasts? Goulden said it was very indistinct, and it took two or three blasts to establish that it *was* a fog signal. Subsequently it was found that it was the signal from the Cape Raso lighthouse near Cape Roca.

Because the foghorn was faint, the Captain thought he was further along the coast, much further out to sea, and ordered the ship to reduce speed and turn to starboard, heading north to enter Cascais Bay to meet the pilot boat. There were various changes of speed and heading, the reasons for which were never fully explained, and at 9.53am the ship was three miles from the coast and heading directly for it at half speed.

Echo-soundings were reported up to 10.10am, the last one being 13 fathoms. At that time the *Hildebrand* was travelling at approximately 9 knots. Then the Captain saw waves breaking on the shoreline. He ordered "Emergency full-astern" and the wheel hard-a-starboard and then, thinking the tide would affect the ship, he ordered hard-a-port. "Looking back on it," Captain Williams said, "had I kept hard to starboard, I would have got clear." The ship began to go to port, "then seemed to come right round," reported the Third Officer. Two minutes later, she hit the rocks, with Cape Raso bearing 315^0 one mile away, in front of Fort St Jorge at Oitavos, Cascais. Captain Williams was so sure he had travelled further than this along the coast that after the grounding, attempts were still being made to identify their location by reference to Fort Velho, some three or four miles further east on the other side of Cascais.

The Enquiry stated that there were three indications of the ship's position that the Captain should have used.

First, the fog signal from Cape Raso could not at first be recognised. When it was recognised as a two-blast signal, the Captain asked Goulden to consult the *Admiralty List of Lights,* which confirmed it was from Cape Raso. But the Captain was so sure that Cascais was just on his port bow (three miles east of his actual position) that he disregarded this sign.

Second, the Captain and Goulden gave evidence that fog was lying close to the horizon and that high land could be seen above it with the skyline clearly visible. Neither took time to consult *The West Coasts of Spain and Portugal Pilot* charts, which clearly show the aspect of the land. This document included a panoramic view of the entrance to the Tagus (the compilers being aware of the nature of fogs in this area), which is vastly different from the skyline as viewed from where the *Hildebrand* grounded.

Moreover, the echo-soundings were not noted in any meaningful way by the Captain. There was a rapid shoaling starting just before ten o'clock, documented from 42 fathoms to 13 fathoms. Captain Williams stated he had not heard the last two soundings of 18 and 13 fathoms; they were reported but must have "fallen on deaf ears," as he was expecting the fog to lift. He reported that he was waiting for the 20-fathom line to be reached, at which time he would turn away.

The Court was forced to the conclusion that because the Captain had completely failed to realise the position of his ship, the accident was due to "the wrongful act or default of the master". In evidence Captain Williams said he had been on his feet for three days and three nights. Due to tiredness and his admitted feeling of overconfidence, he was solely responsible for the disaster. Mr Adams QC said, "What was passing through the mind of the master during the last half-hour before the stranding must remain obscure. There is good evidence that he was a tired man and on his own evidence he was overconfident."

Mr Brandon, representing Captain Williams, said, "The reason for this aberration was overtiredness. While that is not justification it is at least a human reason when we find a man of his experience doing something which is almost crazy."

Concerning the Second Officer, Goulden, the Court recognised that he was working under considerable difficulties, trying to obtain a fix by direction-finder bearings. However they commented that he showed a lack of imagination in helping the Captain to ascertain the ship's position. "In the opinion of this court," they continued, "this officer has good qualities and potentialities and it is to be hoped that the lessons of this disaster will steady him and make him a more resourceful seaman during the course of his future career."

The Enquiry also noted that the Booth Line had decided not to equip their ships with radar, but if the *Hildebrand* had been so fitted, and if the radar had been used properly, they considered that the ship "would hardly have closed the shore in the disastrous manner in which she did."

None of the vessels of the Vestey Group had radar, a fact that even then was barely believable. Why was this? It is rumoured that one of Vestey's ships, a Baltic clipper of the Blue Star Line, had hit the breakwater while going in to Leghorn in Italy. The navigation relied on radar but the officer had misread the device, having it on an incorrect scale. Allegedly, Lord Vestey then removed all radar from their ships. One crewmember of the *Hildebrand* recounted that Lord Vestey had said that radar made the deck officers lazy. When the Formal

Enquiry blamed the grounding in part to the lack of radar, the Vestey group was not pleased. However, following this incident it became essential for every ship to carry radar.

In addition, the Enquiry noted that the patent log was not used. This navigational aid is a torpedo-shaped instrument with rotary fins that is dragged from the stern of a vessel to measure the speed or distance travelled, and is particularly useful in foggy conditions. They considered that, although the grounding was not necessarily caused by the lack of this instrument, if it had been used it would have provided further information to help assess the position of the ship, especially with fluctuating speeds. "By the decision of the master or through indifference (the evidence would support either view) the patent log was not in use."

The Enquiry suspended Williams' Master's certificate for only 12 months dating from the day of the grounding, "... recognising his previous record in peace and war." In tribute to Captain Williams, Mr. Adams QC stated that "his bearing in court, during what must have been for him a painful investigation, was dignified and honourable and he did not seek at any time to cast blame upon others." However, they recommended that he should be granted a certificate of competency as First Mate if he wished to apply for one. This demotion must have been a dreadful blow to a man whom everyone regarded highly and considered a competent mariner.

There was much sympathy among the crew for this "lovely man" (whom they affectionately called "Dizzy Williams"), especially given that the *Hildebrand* had no radar. One crew member related how he had last seen the Captain on the bridge when he thanked the men who volunteered to stay with the vessel. "He was heartbroken about the wreck," he said, adding "He was a great chap."

Afterwards, according to his nephew, Williams was a broken man. He took a shore position with the Mersey Docks & Harbour Board, where he remained until he retired, never going to sea again. However, it has also been reported that he was employed as First Officer by the Harrison Line. Thomas Williams died a few years into his retirement.

Plates recovered from the seabed

CHAPTER 11

EPILOGUE

Such were the tragic events surrounding the *Hildebrand III*. In the years since, divers from diving centres around Cascais have been aware of various shipwrecks scattered along their coastline, including that of the *Hildebrand*. One diver, Pedro Tomas, was inspired to investigate the remains of this ship further, and contacted me.

Tomas, in his late thirties and a project manager in an energy enterprise initiative, was a hobby diver with Exclusive Divers in Cascais. Raised and living in nearby Sintra, he had spent many hours over the years in the area's coastal waters, becoming an expert and well-respected sub-aqua diver.

Divers had known for many years that pieces of the wreck of the *Hildebrand* lay at the sea bottom, and had heard stories from local people and fishermen about seeing the stranding in 1957. Pedro Tomas wanted to know more. I sent him a copy of the Formal Enquiry and, together with my memories, this provided the missing information in the story of the ship's demise.

He and a diver friend, a very able sub-aqua cameraman, Pedro Carvalho, decided to make a film of the *Hildebrand's* shipwreck story. This required filming in the area of the ship's final resting place - but the waters there are not for novice divers. Tomas says, "In any one year, one can count on one's fingers the times when conditions are excellent for diving." The area is predominantly sand, with rocks that become progressively larger nearer the coast. The seas can be extremely rough, churning up the sandbed and making visibility difficult. On a good, calm day visibility can be up to 15 metres, but at the other extreme can be as poor as only 2 metres. The depth varies between 8 and 11 metres depending on the tide and position of the

Pedro de Carvalho (left) & Pedro Tomas

Hildebrand's artefacts.

More than 50 years on, due to the initial salvage work and the strong sea currents at the site, little remains of the ship. However, divers can still see parts of the hull, with its openings and hatchways, part of a mast, and plates. There are various other pieces of the ship lying on the seabed, including taps and other hardware.

For his film, Pedro Carvalho interviewed a number of people associated with both the shipwreck and the finding of the wreck parts, including Engineer Tony McClements, fire officers, fishermen, divers, me and other witnesses; he also obtained some footage from the local newsreels. The film was shown to the public in various venues in the Lisbon area, to great acclaim. It is a lasting tribute to this majestic and well-loved cruise liner whose days ended so tragically.

BIBLIOGRAPHY

Astley, P.,   personal communication, 2011

Astley, R.,   personal communication, 2011

Austin, F.,   personal communication, 2012

Baker, H.,   personal communication, 2011

Carvalho, P., personal communication, 2009

Catholic Herald, "Shipwreck Cost Them £900", letter to
          editor from Rev. T. Winder & Rt Rev. Mgr
          James Canon, 11 October 1957

Catholic Herald, "£904 for 'Hildebrand' Students", 27
          December 1957

Clark, G.,   personal communication, 2012

Cowell, E.,   letter to *Sea Breezes* (August 2009)

Daily Mail,   "Passengers sing Hymns in Holed Liner", 25
          September 1957

Daily Telegraph, "Liner Captain Admits he was
          Over-Confident", 4 February 1958

Daily Telegraph, "Master Blamed for Liner Loss", 7
          February 1958

Davies, H.,   personal communication, 2011

Evans, G.,   personal communication, 2011

Gilbert, D.,   personal communication, 2012

Gillen, J.,   personal communication, 2011

H.M.S.O.,   The Merchant Shipping Act, 1894: Report of Court (No. 8000) R.M.S. "Hildebrand" O.N. 185422, 1958

Harman, J., personal communication, 2011

Harrison, E., personal communication, 2011

Hilton, P.,   personal communication, 2011

Jones, F.J., personal communication, 2011

Jordan, J.,   "S.S. Hildebrand", letter to *Sea Breezes, (September 2009)*

Liverpool Daily Post, "Mersey ship on rocks in fog", 26 September 1957

Liverpool Daily Post, "Stranded Hildebrand may be total loss", 10 October 1957

Liverpool Daily Post, "Over-Confident Says Hildebrand's Master", 4 February 1958

Liverpool Daily Post, "Hildebrand's Master Accepts Blame for Stranding", 6 February 1958

Liverpool Daily Post, "Hildebrand's Master's Certificate Suspended for 12 months", 7 February 1958

Liverpool Echo, "Ship Breaks Back", 2 December 1958

Liverpool Evening Express, "Liner afire in Liverpool dock"
20 April 1957

Lockyer, D., personal diary 1957

Lockyer, J.K.,personal diary 1957

Lockyer, J.K.,"Shipwreck", *The Kingdom Overseas*
(1958) pp93-95

Lockyer, R., "The Shipwreck of SS 'Hildebrand' 1957",
Sea Breezes (May 2009), pp192-94.

Mawdsley, J., personal communication, 2011

McClements, A., personal communication, 2010

O'Hara, F.,   personal communication, 2011

Parracho, J.L., personal communication, 2010

Peate, D.,   "Memories of Sunken Ship", letter to
County Times, 4 January 2008

Potier, P.,   personal communication, 2011

Ribiero, S.,   personal communication, 2010

Robinson, R.C.G., personal communication, 2011

Selby Times, "First journey out of Yorkshire and then…
Shipwreck!" September 1987

Smith, A., comment on log of www.bluestarline.org, 2
October 2009

Snow, A., "Superstitious Sailors who Blamed Sinking on a
Cat", *County Times,* 15 February 2008

Tetlow, S., "Liner on a Lee Shore", *Sea Breezes*,
(December 1957)

The Times, "British Liner Aground", 26 September 1957

The Times, "Ship's Hull Holed", 26 September 1957

The Times, "Pamir Inquiry Opens", 30 September 1957

Thurlow, A.J., personal communication, 2011

Tomas, P.,   personal communication, 2009

Tomas, P. & Lockyer, R., "RMS Hildebrand 3",
Planetad'agua (November/December
2009) pp68-73

Watson, G., personal communication, 2011

Williams, B., personal communication, 2011

Wirth, H.G., "The Last Voyage of the Pamir", *Reader's
Digest* (June 1958), pp25-30